PAUL HINDLE

MEDIEVAL ROADS AND TRACKS

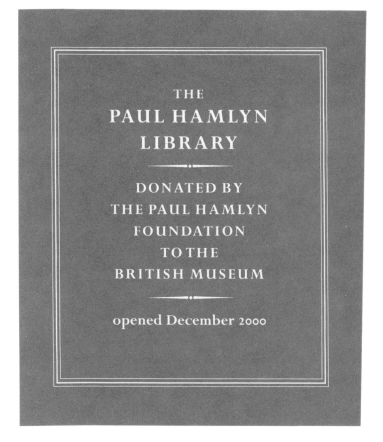

SHIRE ARCHAEOLOGY

Cover illustration
Part of the Gough map, drawn about 1360, showing south-east England. East is at the
top, and London is the prominent town with roads radiating from it in all directions.

British Library Cataloguing in Publication Data:
Hindle, Brian Paul
Medieval roads and tracks. – (Shire archaeology; no. 26)
1. Roads – England – history
I. Title
388.1'0942'0902
ISBN 0 7478 0390 0

Published in 2002 by
SHIRE PUBLICATIONS LTD
Cromwell House, Church Street, Princes Risborough,
Buckinghamshire HP27 9AA, UK.

Series Editor: James Dyer.

Number 26 in the Shire Archaeology series.

ISBN 0 7478 0390 0.

First published 1982
Second edition 1989
Third edition 1998; reprinted 2002

Printed in Great Britain by
CIT Printing Services Ltd, Press Buildings,
Merlins Bridge, Haverfordwest, Pembrokeshire SA61 1XF.

Contents

ACKNOWLEDGEMENTS
The maps were drawn by Gustav Dobrzynski, cartographer in the Department of Geography, University of Salford; the author is grateful for his cartographic clarity.

Figures 18 to 22, 28, 36, 38 and 41 are reproduced by permission of the Committee for Aerial Archaeology, University of Cambridge. Figures 23 and 29 were taken by Richard W. Bagshawe, figure 34 by John Steane, and the remainder (except figure 30) by the author.

List of illustrations

1

Introduction

The medieval period in England saw a massive growth in all sections of economic life: population increased, towns grew, industry blossomed and trade, which was both a cause and an effect of this growth, became vitally important. Not only was agricultural produce such as grain and wool moved from field to market but also such diverse items as stone, metal, wood, woollen cloth and a whole range of industrial products needed transporting. However, this growth of the economy was not continuous; probably beginning with the political stability after 1066 under William I, it tended to stagnate in times of civil unrest such as the reigns of Stephen (1135-54) and John (1199-1216), but certain periods stand out as having experienced more rapid growth, notably the century after John's reign. A period of stagnation followed the poor harvests of 1313-16, and this was made much worse by the arrival of the Black Death in 1348, which reduced the population by forty per cent. A long and painfully slow recovery period followed, and it was not until the accession of the Tudors in 1485 that growth recommenced. This marked the beginning of the end of the medieval period, which concluded in 1536-40 with the dissolution of the monasteries. They had maintained the medieval way of life, particularly in the more remote areas of northern and western England.

Such was the political and economic background to medieval England. Although relatively few people needed to travel it was vitally important for the whole economy that it was possible for both people and produce to travel easily when required. For goods there were clearly two alternatives: they could travel by boat or by road. Bulky produce in particular tended to be moved by river or by sea, but most parts of England and Wales did not have this option, as they had no navigable rivers or had rivers that were obstructed by low bridges, weirs or fish traps.

Thus roads must have formed the backbone of the transport system. And yet it is curious that so little has been written about these roads which were so fundamental to England's economic growth. Writers on this topic have largely confined themselves to looking at travellers, road maintenance, the means and safety of travel and the state of the roads. There has been little or no attempt to see *where* the roads were, that is, to view the roads as an integrated network. The reason for this is probably the lack of information available, for virtually no new roads were constructed during this period, and it is very difficult to ascribe a date to a road which was not actually built, but which just came into use. C. T. Flower, writing in 1923, coined the memorable phrase that these roads which grew from habitual lines of travel 'made and maintained themselves'.

There was already a road system in existence, at least 16,000 km (10,000 miles) of Roman roads, built mainly by AD 150, but which had not been maintained for well over six hundred years by the time of the Norman Conquest. Many of these roads remained in use, providing a basic network. But many of the new towns of medieval England, such as Oxford, Coventry or Plymouth, were not on Roman roads and so new roads must have been needed to serve them, as well as the myriad villages in between.

The nature of these new medieval roads differed from that of Roman or modern roads; essentially the road was not a physical entity, a thin strip of land with definite boundaries; rather it was a right of way, an 'easement', with both legal and customary status, leading from one village or town to the next. If the route was much frequented it became a physical track, with two important provisos. The first was that if the road was obstructed or had become 'foundrous' in wet weather, then the traveller had the right to diverge from the road, even if that entailed trampling crops; this was enshrined in law in the Statute of Winchester in 1285. The second proviso was that where the road had to climb a hill or bank then multiple tracks would develop, the traveller taking the easiest route then available. Most of the surviving sections of medieval roads come in this category, where roads left cultivated land and the tracks have thus not been ploughed out or otherwise destroyed.

A few new roads were built; in 1278 Roger Mortimer was charged by Edward I to enlarge and widen the roads and passes into parts of north Wales, in connection with the campaigns against the Welsh. The three causeways connecting Ely with the rest of England across the fenlands are perhaps the largest medieval road building works, but the earliest charters do not refer specifically to the construction of these causeways and there is the possibility that they too could be of Roman origin.

Several royal statutes of various dates made requirements about the width of roads and of the land to be cleared on either side – but often more in the interests of safety from outlaws than of improving the roads. The four great highways (Watling Street, Ermine Street, Fosse Way and Icknield Way) were always regarded as being under the king's special protection, which supports the idea that the Roman roads remained in use in the medieval period.

The greatest problem in attempting to trace medieval roads is that if the route is no longer in use then, not having been engineered, it will largely have disappeared. On the other hand, if it has remained in use it will have had a more modern road constructed on top, burying or destroying any archaeological evidence of the medieval road. In order to trace medieval roads, therefore, one must begin in the library rather than in the field. There is written evidence in the form of medieval maps, travellers' records and place-names which can help us to see which Roman roads remained in use and where medieval roads came into use. All this evidence will help us to link together the widely scattered and difficult to date archaeological remains. This book must thus devote a good deal of attention to the sources of information on medieval roads rather than concentrating on the often dubious physical remains, for virtually the only way to confirm field evidence of a medieval road is to demonstrate from the historical record that it was in use during that period. A medieval road may have originally come into use in pre-Roman, Roman, Saxon or medieval times, but we must have evidence for its use between say 1066 and 1485; when it first came into being is of little importance.

2

Travel in medieval times

Medieval travellers

It used to be thought that few people travelled out of their own town or village in medieval times. Most people certainly travelled far less than they do today, but the notion of a peasant spending the whole of his or her life in one place is not necessarily correct. At the start of the medieval period, with the imposition of the feudal system, peasants were not free to leave their manor permanently, though they would doubtless know their local market town well. After the Black Death had reduced the population, there was a shortage of labour and people started to move to find better paid work; these paid workers were outside the feudal system, which was by then in rapid decline.

J.J. Jusserand in his classic book *English Wayfaring Life in the Middle Ages* devotes most of his attention to various travellers, both lay and religious. In addition to workmen he includes minstrels, messengers, merchants and outlaws in the first category and preachers, friars, pardoners and pilgrims in the second. He could also have included bishops, travelling justices, sheriffs, revenue collectors and kings. Kings are a special case because it is possible to trace their movements, often on a day-to-day basis.

The itineraries for the kings, which were compiled from letters they wrote, charters they granted or simply from the details of their household accounts, are the most useful, for from the time of King John onwards we have an almost complete record of each king's whereabouts. More than that, the entire court was itinerant and moved with the king, certainly until well into the fourteenth century. Thus the baggage train, comprising from ten to twenty carts and wagons, containing everything from the treasury to the king's wardrobe, had to move about with the king and must have required adequate roads. The kings were almost constantly on the move, and there are few recorded complaints about the condition of the roads.

Certain types of trade on the road led to some roads being given special names, such as Maltway, Oxdrove, Sheepdrove and Saltway. These roads were not specifically constructed for these uses but were named after the type of traffic which often used them. The roads leading from the inland salt towns (*wiches*), including Droitwich, Nantwich, Middlewich and Northwich, are well known, and their courses can usually be traced by 'salt' place-names such as Saltersford and Saltersgate.

A 'portway' led to a particular port or market town. These were usually prehistoric tracks or Roman roads being used again. Many continued to be called portways during the medieval period. The *Anglo-Saxon Chronicle* mentions the portway from Northampton to Southampton via Oxford, and a well-known example is the Roman road from Silchester to Old Sarum (Salisbury); it is no longer a through route, and its use near the abandoned Roman town of Silchester must have ceased early in Saxon times. In Derbyshire, a portway can be traced from Nottingham to Wirksworth and Bakewell by a succession of documentary references and place names.

A road thought to have been used by the army was known as a 'herepath' (*here* being Old English for army). A good example is the Salisbury Way, leading from Shaftesbury via White Sheet Hill and Chiselbury to Salisbury. Its origins are probably prehistoric, but it is mentioned as a herepath and boundary in two Anglo-Saxon charters, it was used as a drove road and eventually it became part of the main coach road to the west from Salisbury. It is now a quiet green lane (figures 1 and 2). The Wiltshire Herepath is another well preserved

1. This deeply entrenched holloway ascending White Sheet Hill, Wiltshire, was named as a herepath in an Anglo-Saxon charter and later became a drove road and a coach road. Traffic now follows the A30 in the valley below.

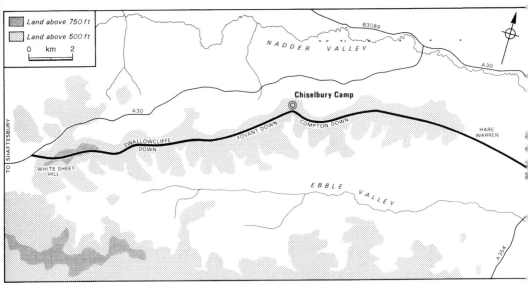

2. The Salisbury Way, Wiltshire, has probably been in use since prehistoric times.

trackway which runs from Marlborough to Avebury over Fyfield Down, but it too probably has prehistoric origins, effectively being a branch of the Great Ridgeway. It was also used until the eighteenth century as a coach road.

Other place-name elements can give clues to old routes; *way* is probably the commonest, but *stretten, heol, fford* and *gate* can all refer to a road, coming from Latin, Welsh, Welsh and Danish respectively. Any word having a connection with roads derived from any of these languages can suggest the line of a former road. We shall see how place-name elements can be used as collaborative evidence in the study of a local area later in the book.

Church and corpse roads

A few tracks were used primarily for access to the parish church. Sometimes documentary evidence survives; in the accounts of the Bailiff of the Forest of Dartmoor for 1491, a parcel of land is described as bounded by a 'churchway' to Widecombe. In the extreme south-west of Cornwall (West Penwith) these ways have been identified as 'church paths', many of which are named as such in documents, often in the Cornish equivalent, 'forth eglos' (usually shortened to 'freglos'). In medieval times, this area had only 13 parish churches, and church paths led to them from outlying farmsteads up to 5 km (3 miles) away. Many of the paths were marked by granite wayside crosses. Over a hundred of these crosses remain, though others have been lost and are represented only by field names.

A more bizarre type of road was that known as a 'corpse road'. In

3. The villagers of Mardale Green, Cumbria (normally submerged beneath Haweswater), had to carry their dead via this corpse road over the fells for burial at Shap until 1736.

many parts of England, particularly in the more remote areas, the establishment of churches did not keep pace with the growth of population. Thus enormous parishes survived, and although there were usually several subsidiary chapels in these large parishes, only the parish church would have had the right of burial, and consequently the dead had to be carried there to be buried. Kendal (Cumbria) was such a parish; it extended to include not only what is now Bowness-on-Windermere but also Ambleside and Grasmere over 25 km (16 miles) from the parish church. Perhaps the large number of deaths by plague in 1348-9 hastened the creation of new parishes of Grasmere and Windermere in those years. Corpse roads sometimes carried little other traffic in remote areas; the villagers of Mardale Green (now flooded by Haweswater) took their dead on horseback some 10 km (6 miles) over Mardale Common and down Swindale for burial at Shap. The chapel at Mardale was granted its own burial ground in 1728, and the last corpse was taken to Shap in 1736 (figure 3). Ordnance Survey maps show another Lake District corpse road from Wasdale Head, across Burnmoor to Boot in Eskdale.

There are several such tracks in the highlands of Scotland, including routes from Glen Strath Farrar to Kintail, from Quoich Bridge to Glen Shiel, and from Glen Garry to Glen Moriston. Less than 16 km (10 miles) south of Edinburgh, a 'kirk road' runs from Bavelaw and Loganlee across the pass between Carnethy and Scald Law (the highest point of the Pentland Hills) to the church at Penicuik.

Examples in northern England include a corpse road which runs from Garrigill (in the south Tyne valley above Alston) for 18 km (11 miles), reaching a height of almost 800 metres (2600 feet) on Cross Fell, before descending to the mother church at Kirkland in the Eden valley. Only a few miles to the south there is a parallel route from Birkdale in upper Teesdale, which runs for 20 km (12 miles), passing through the great gash of High Cup to the parish church at Dufton. The track through the chasm is known as Narrowgate, and the whole route is still in use as it is now followed by the Pennine Way. Further south, in Swaledale, bodies were carried in wicker baskets from the area around Keld at the top of the dale, for over 20 km (12 miles) to the church at Grinton, until a burial ground was provided at Muker in 1580. In Derbyshire, the dead from Edale were taken over Hollins Cross for burial in Castleton until 1633.

All those who died within the area of the ancient Forest of Dartmoor had to be buried at Lydford until 1260. The people worst affected were those who lived in the centre of the moor, only a few miles from the church at Widecombe. They had to take corpses across the moor, climbing to a height of over 460 metres (1500 feet). Here weather conditions could be so bad that the direct route to Lydford could not be used, and roundabout routes had to be taken instead, which were often twice as long. There are several possible routes across the moor from Two Bridges, Bellever and Postbridge; they traverse the southern slopes of Cut Hill and cross the Tavy near Wapsworthy, 5 km (3 miles) short of Lydford. These roads are known locally as Lich Ways (*lich* or *lych* being an old word for corpse).

Pilgrim routes

In a more pious age than our own, it was common for people to travel to visit the various shrines dotted around the country, as well as those abroad. In England, the shrine of St Swithun at Winchester was much visited, and pilgrims also travelled to remote places to seek a particular saint's aid. But the principal pilgrim destinations were the long-established chapel of Our Lady of Walsingham and, later, the shrine of Thomas à Becket in Canterbury, set up after his murder in 1170.

At the start of *The Canterbury Tales,* written in about 1400, Chaucer says that once April comes,

> Than longen folk to goon on pilgrimages ....
> And specially from every shires ende
> Of Engelond to Caunterbury they wende ...

His pilgrims travelled from Southwark, and only five places en route are mentioned (Depeford, Grenewych, Sidyngborne, Boghtoun under Blee and Bobbe-up-and-doun; the last is probably Harbledown). Although Chaucer uses the pilgrimage to string together a set of tales, he takes it for granted that his readers know the road, and he never mentions any difficulties of travel. We may assume that this Roman road was still in a reasonable state of repair. This was surely the most important single pilgrim route in later medieval England, and the road was equally important as part of the main route to Dover and thence to France.

One particular route has become known as the Pilgrims' Way. It runs along the North Downs, beginning at Winchester, and proceeds via Alton to Farnham, then along the Hog's Back past Guildford, then to Dorking, Titsey, Wrotham, Snodland, Charing and finally to Canterbury. In fact this is probably a route of much greater antiquity and importance, its use long pre-dating the coming of pilgrims. Hilaire Belloc called it the Old Road, and it is a typical prehistoric ridgeway route. It may well have provided access to the great ceremonial centres of Salisbury Plain. The original route from Stonehenge passed where Andover and Basingstoke now stand and joined the Pilgrims' Way at Farnham; this older route is known as the Harrow Way. Several Roman villas appear to be connected with the Pilgrims' Way, though there is no evidence of the route being improved by the Romans.

Unfortunately, there is no real evidence for the use of this route by medieval pilgrims and the first mention of this romantic idea dates from the eighteenth century. In any case, the traffic of pilgrims lasted for less than 400 years, and the track probably has its origins some 3500 years ago. No doubt some pilgrims did use it, but its main users would have been drovers and traders, especially in the eighteenth century when they were trying to avoid the tolls of the newly turnpiked roads. It is always dubious to name a track after one particular type of user; only rarely was any road used for a single purpose.

Nevertheless, the passage of men and animals over thousands of years has created a very clear series of tracks and holloways (entrenched roads) along this route. Sometimes the route runs on top of the ridge, but more frequently it appears as a terrace way on the scarp slope, as parts of the chalk ridge are topped with clay-with-flints which would have been hard going in wet conditions. Some sections are overlain by modern roads, whilst others remain as tracks or paths. It has been an important through route for thousands of years, and the 'Old Road' is certainly a better name for it. More recently, the North Downs Way has been established as one of the many long-distance footpaths; its route has been chosen to avoid motor roads as much as possible and coincides only in places with the various lines of the Old Road or the Pilgrims' Way.

Monastic routes

There are many tracks with monastic connections which seem to suggest a medieval origin. One such is the so-called Abbots' Way across southern Dartmoor which appears to connect Buckfast Abbey with the abbeys at Tavistock and Buckland. However, the track is certainly older than the abbeys, and although the monks no doubt used it, it was always known as the Jobbers' Path or Cawse until a traveller called John Andrews first dubbed it the Abbots' Way in 1794. A parallel route some miles further north across the moor, which is marked with 22 stone crosses, appears to be a much better candidate as a monastic route; however, there is no direct evidence of monks using this track either.

Rather more successful has been the detailed investigation of the numerous routes connected with Strata Florida Abbey in Cardiganshire by Colyer. The Welsh place-names include an 'abbey road', 'pilgrims' ford' and 'monks' way'. Colyer's study was backed up by detailed field observation and historical research.

In the Yorkshire Dales the most famous surviving monastic road is probably Mastiles Lane, which was originally known as Strete Gate. It runs from Kilnsey (a grange or farm of Fountains Abbey) westwards across Malham Moor, heading for Ribblesdale and Clapham, and eventually for the abbey's distant estates in the Lake District. Rights of passage were granted to the abbey's men, animals and goods throughout its length. Originally it was an unwalled track across the open moors, marked by crosses at prominent points; several of their bases are still in place. Mastiles Lane continued to be used by the drovers, driving their cattle from Scotland. When the whole area was eventually enclosed in the late eighteenth and early nineteenth centuries, it and numerous other drovers' routes were constrained between new walls which were built sufficiently far apart to allow easy passage for the herds of cattle. It is now one of the many 'green roads' of the Pennines (figure 4).

Drove roads

Although cattle droving reached its peak in the mid-nineteenth century, its origins may well be prehistoric, and the trade was well established in the medieval period. A good example is a road just south of the Lune Gorge in Cumbria, referred to in a late twelfth-century charter as

4. This bleak monastic route, Mastiles Lane, above Wharfedale in North Yorkshire, is at a height of almost 400 metres (1300 feet). In summer at least it is a 'green road'.

Galwaithegate (i.e. the Galloway Road). A parallel road 20 km (12 miles) further east is still named Galloway Gate on the 1:25,000 Ordnance Survey map (figures 5 and 6).

Locally animals were driven from country to town, and nationally from the north and west of Britain to the south and east. Distinctive drove roads soon emerged, sometimes referred to as 'driftways' or 'green roads'. Across open country they could be wide, as the cattle chose their own course, leaving little evidence of their passing, though in hilly areas there were obvious constraints on the routes they could take. In the lowlands the routes were restricted by fields, and the increasing enclosure of fields constrained the routes still further. Today the surviving drove roads often appear as sinuous wide roads, up to 20 metres (66 feet) wide between walls or hedges, with a narrow strip of tarmac down the middle. But this gives little idea of how they must have looked in the middle ages before enclosure.

Place-names may give further clues; the roads themselves may be named on maps, and the overnight resting and grazing places (stances or halts), usually about 12 to 20 km (7-12 miles) apart, can have distinctive field and pub names, such as Half Penny Field or the Drovers' Rest. In England the pub names can refer to the origin of the cattle, for example Scotch Inn, Craven Heifer and Welsh Arms. The former drovers' inn at Stockbridge in Hampshire still has a sign in Welsh offering good hay, pasture, beer and bed! In the fens there are place-names such as Whaplode Drove and Holbeach Drove.

5. *Galwaithegate* (Galloway Road), Cumbria, was a major link in the network of drove roads between Scotland and northern England; it prospered until the Shap railway was opened in 1846. The M6 now carries most of the traffic.

6. Galloway Gate, North Yorkshire, was one of the drove roads leading south from the Eden valley. In the heyday of droving there were no walls and probably a multitude of parallel tracks.

Surviving examples of drove roads include the track along the Hambleton Hills from Swainby to Sutton Bank in Yorkshire, many of the 'green roads' of the Pennines, the section of the Roman Ermine Street south of Lincoln (known as both High Dyke and The Drift), the Berkshire Ridgeway (Avebury to Goring) and the Salisbury Way from White Sheet Hill towards Salisbury (figures 1 and 2). In the Midlands both the Welsh Road (best seen from Kenilworth to Culworth) and Banbury Lane are typical drove roads in that they tend to avoid villages rather than going through them.

Conditions on the roads

Opinion has long been divided on the state of the roads in medieval England. One school of thought dwells largely on the difficulties of travel, noting that in wet weather the roads became rivers and that in winter they became impassable for wheeled traffic. Indeed Parliament was suspended in 1339 because so many members were held up by the bad weather. On the other hand there is strong evidence that the haulage of heavy goods was undertaken in autumn and winter. For example, stone was transported over 10 km (6 miles) to build Vale Royal Abbey (Cheshire), with the carters making two round trips every day for a month at a time, even in winter; the slack months were May, August and September.

The best information on medieval travellers is contained in the royal itineraries, and these can also be used to see whether travel in the winter was difficult. The kings had to move to collect taxes and to consume dues in kind, and the earlier medieval kings in particular were constantly on the move. King John spent only one month of his entire reign without a move, and that was when he was besieging Rochester Castle in November 1215. He moved, on average, over thirteen times each month throughout his reign, though travelling least in June and October (figure 7).

Edward I was also a great traveller, concerning himself much with affairs in Wales and, later, in Scotland. He averaged almost nine moves each month throughout his reign, favouring August and September and travelling least in November (figure 8). In January 1300 he covered the 575 km (360 miles) from Bamburgh to Windsor in 25 days, including six days when he did not travel. He was thus averaging about 32 km (20 miles) a day; clearly travel in winter presented few problems to the movement of the royal household. The king and his retinue with their horses, wagons and carts represented a not unusual type of traffic on medieval roads. Travel, although slow, was something undertaken as a matter of course, even in winter.

By the end of the medieval period the roads were still in a tolerable condition; John Leland, travelling around 1540, rarely complains of them. William Harrison, however, writing in 1586, says that the highways had deteriorated drastically in the previous twenty years. There are two possible causes for this change; the first was the dissolution of the monasteries in 1536-40, for they had effected much of what little road maintenance was done, and the second was the rapid growth of the Tudor economy. In medieval times the roads had been generally adequate in both quantity and quality for the amount of traffic using them. In the mid sixteenth century it seems that the fine balance between the durability of the roads and the amount of traffic was upset, and it was only then that the roads became unable to cope with the sheer volume of that traffic.

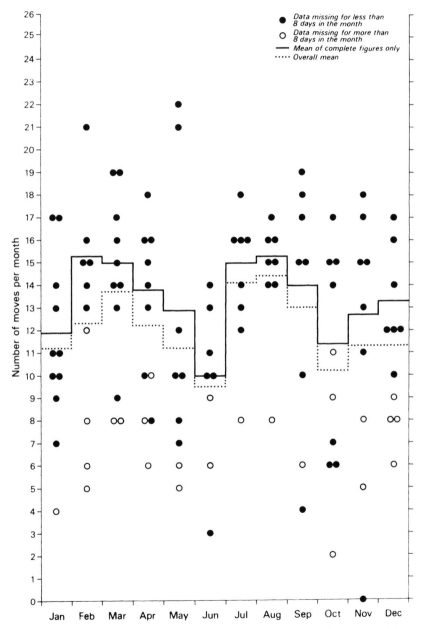

7. King John: number of moves per month. Each month of his reign is represented by a circle; for example, in two separate Januaries he moved seventeen times, and in another January he moved only four times, though this latter figure is based on incomplete evidence. He moved on average over thirteen times a month.

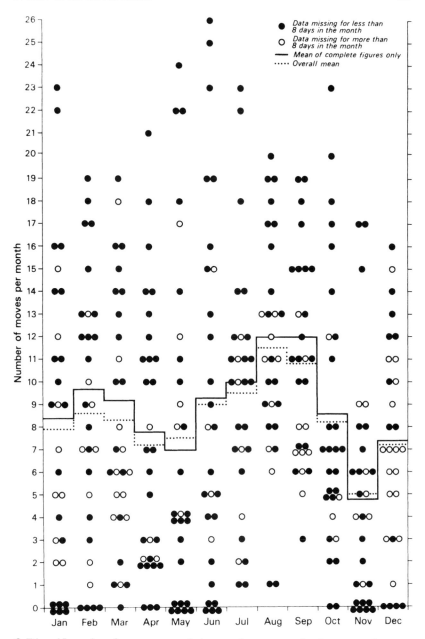

8. Edward I: number of moves per month; he moved on average nine times a month.

3

Documentary evidence

Documentary evidence is sparse and often of a negative kind, such as the references to impassable roads in court cases. Roads or their ditches were frequently blocked; for example, in 1357 the Fosse Way was obstructed with trenches, piles and trees at Belgrave (Leicestershire). In 1386 the Abbot of Chertsey allowed two 'wells' 12 feet (3.7 metres) wide and 8 feet (2.4 metres) deep to exist in the high road from Egham to Staines; an unknown man had drowned and the abbot had claimed his goods! Local enterprise in Norfolk must have been somewhat discouraged when a man was fined for building a new road from Yarmouth to Winterton to replace one blocked with sand.

The scattered references to roads in medieval documents are important in that these specific roads are thus known to have been in use. For example, Holm Cultram Abbey (Cumbria) had a right of way 'by the ordinary road through Bassenthwaite' from 1290 to 1327, and the Roman road from Kendal to Shap is referred to as *magna strata* (great street), *magna via* (great way) and *stayngate* (paved road) at various times during the medieval period. In 1354 Bishop Welton promised forty days of remitted penance for anyone working on a boggy stretch of road at Wragmyre between Carlisle and Penrith. It is unusual for a road (rather than a bridge) to be the subject of such an indulgence.

Further south, an inquest in Suffolk in 1364 requested the Lord of Bildeston to clean two ditches on the road to Nedging, and in 1285 Edward I wrote to the prior of Dunstable ordering him to repair the high roads through Dunstable (probably Watling Street and the Icknield Way):

> Because we have learnt that the high roads, which stretch through the middle of your vill aforesaid, are so broken up and deep by the frequent passage of carts, that dangerous injuries continuously threaten those passing by those roads: we wishing to be guarded against such injuries, which by that fault will be able to happen in the future unless the remedy be more speedily applied, command you that you, that is to say, each one of you according to his estate and capabilities, shall cause those roads to be filled in and mended, as in such case it has been accustomed to be done in times past. So that for default of you in this part it shall not be necessary for us to apply a heavier hand to this. (From the annals of Dunstable Priory, translated by K. C. Newton, 1866.)

The movement of bulky produce has left few records, and it was only when the government became involved with such trade that records have survived. In particular, records were kept for the provisioning of the kings' armies; the accounts give details of the goods bought or requisitioned and the type of transport used to take the goods to the customs ports for shipment to Wales, Scotland or France. The best surviving records are those for Lincolnshire and Yorkshire; here goods were moved to progressively larger centres, eventually by river – it should be remembered that these two counties are well served by rivers, which does not apply to most of England. Records also survive for the various Cistercian monasteries which moved their wool to distant ports chiefly by packhorse or cart. Such long hauls as those from Furness Abbey (Cumbria) to Beverley (East Yorkshire), Holm Cultram (Cumbria) to Newcastle upon Tyne, and Vale Royal (Cheshire) to London or Boston (Lincolnshire) suggest that these long distances were not unduly difficult. The detailed routes, however, are not known.

Itineraries

The various itineraries of the medieval period provide evidence of the movement of individual people, and, by implication, of the simple physical existence of roads. There is, for example, the itinerary of Giraldus Cambrensis (Gerald of Wales), who toured Wales in 1188 with Archbishop Baldwin, and a great many bishops' itineraries survive from the mid thirteenth century onwards. Unfortunately the bishops visited only a few places, and detail is usually lacking. Occasionally records of the movements of private individuals were kept; the best known is the route recorded by Robert of Nottingham, who was buying wheat for the king in 1324-5 in the area around the river Trent.

The most complete itineraries, however, are those compiled posthumously for the kings, who visited a wide range of places, from castles to manors and abbeys to market towns. Problems arise in the interpretation of these itineraries, principally where information is lacking, but once the routes are plotted on a map it is reasonable to suppose that if a king (and his court) used certain routes frequently, then some reasonable track or road must have existed. The routes taken by John, Edward I and Edward II are shown in figures 9, 10 and 11. In each case there are two maps, the first showing all the routes travelled, and the second showing only those travelled three times or more.

King John (figure 9) was noted even in his own time as a great traveller; he carried his scrutiny into the far north and west where kings seldom went – indeed his visit to Carlisle in February 1201 was the first time that any king had been to that area since William II wrested the land from the Scots in 1092. John was probably too efficient an administrator for his time (his predecessor, Richard I, had spent only

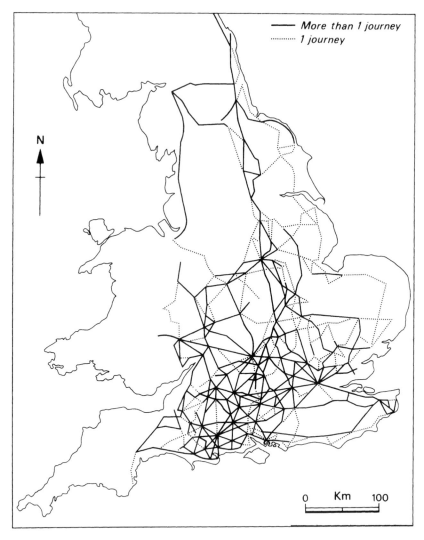

9. The itinerary of King John. The map above shows all his journeys, whilst that on the opposite page shows only routes he travelled three times or more.

six months of his ten-year reign in England), and although many state records start during his reign and we can therefore trace his movements accurately, this efficiency no doubt helped his ultimate downfall. Sometimes there are gaps in his itinerary, such as on his second visit to

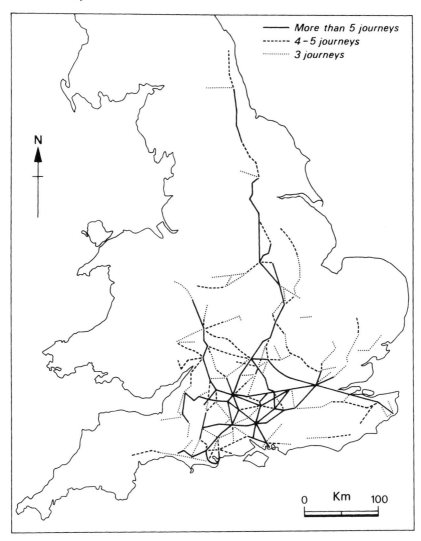

More than 5 journeys
4 - 5 journeys
3 journeys

N

0   Km   100

Carlisle in 1206, when he is last recorded in the city on 20th February and next appears in Chester on 1st March. It is impossible to say which route he took; on figure 9 the route is shown via Kendal and Lancaster, though he could equally well have gone by sea! Happily there are few gaps of this magnitude.

Edward I's itinerary (figure 10) shows twice as many journeys as that

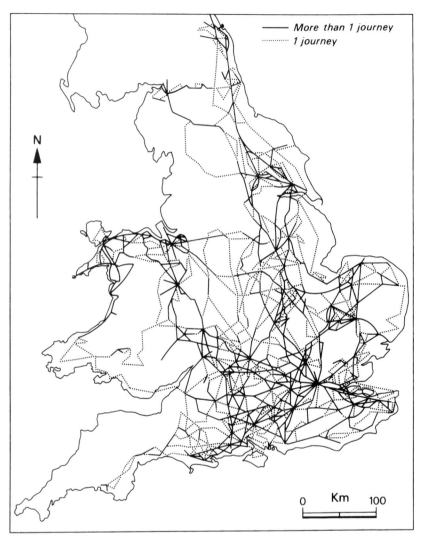

10. The itinerary of Edward I. The map above shows all his journeys, whilst that on the opposite page shows only routes he travelled three times or more.

for John; in particular he travelled to Wales and Scotland, though his routes beyond the Scottish border are not shown on the maps. Perhaps the most curious aspect of his travels is how little he used the same routes, suggesting perhaps that cross-country travel presented few

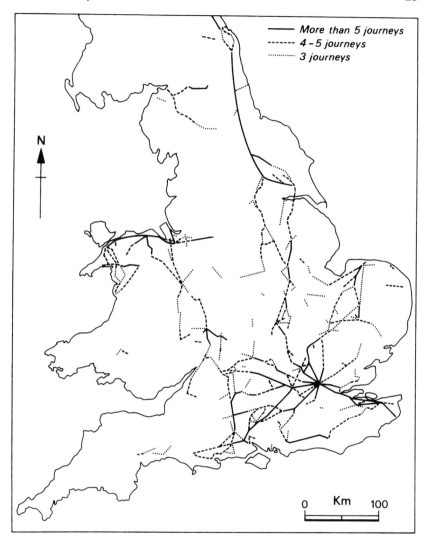

problems. Edward II (figure 11) also covered very few routes more than
twice. However, his route to the north stands out clearly: it ran along
Watling Street to Kings Langley and Stony Stratford and then proceeded
through Northampton, Leicester, Nottingham, Doncaster, Pontefract,
York, Northallerton, Darlington, Durham and Newcastle to Berwick. In
addition Edward seems to have travelled by boat on the Trent and the

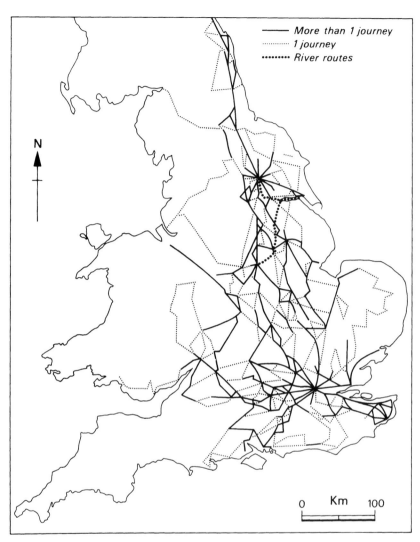

11. The itinerary of Edward II. The map above shows all his journeys, whilst that on the opposite page shows only routes he travelled three times or more.

Ouse; he could equally have used the Thames, but his mode of transport is impossible to ascertain from the itinerary. An attempt has been made to condense these maps into one which shows all the routes travelled four times or more by more than one of the three medieval kings whose travels have been plotted (figure 12). Clearly they travelled mostly in central and southern England, avoiding Wales (apart from Edward I), the north-west, the south-west and, perhaps more surprisingly, East

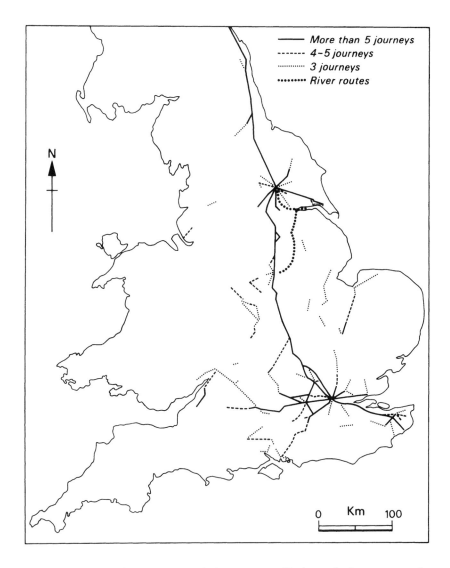

———— More than 5 journeys
------- 4–5 journeys
············ 3 journeys
•••••••• River routes

N

0   Km   100

Anglia, an area of great economic importance. Perhaps the later monarchs remembered the loss of King John's baggage train in the silt of the Wash after leaving King's Lynn in October 1216.

A particularly interesting itinerary is a list of routes from the Premonstratensian abbey of Titchfield in Hampshire to each of the other houses of the same order of canons, as far distant as Alnwick and Shap, passing through many major towns en route (figure 13). The manuscript dates from about 1400 and complements the routes depicted on the Gough map (see chapter 4).

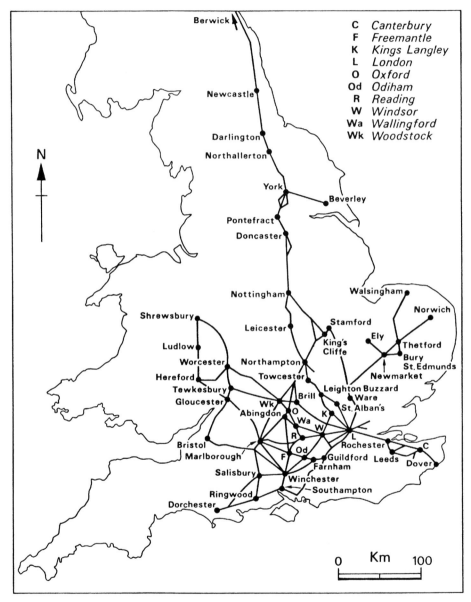

12. The royal itinerary network. This map shows a basic route network which would have been used most often by the three kings John, Edward I and Edward II.

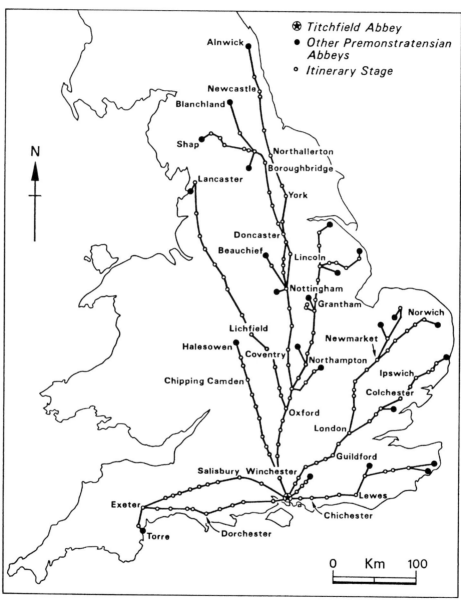

13. Titchfield itinerary routes.

14. The Matthew Paris map of Britain (version A), drawn in 1250, shows a single route from Dover to Newcastle.

4

Map evidence

If the archaeological and documentary evidence is poor and uneven, we are fortunate in having several medieval maps showing roads on a national scale. Matthew Paris, a monk at St Albans, drew four maps of Britain in about 1250 which are based on an itinerary from Dover to Newcastle (figure 14). The route forms the backbone of the maps and goes by way of Canterbury, Rochester, London, St Albans, Dunstable, Northampton, Leicester, Belvoir (a cell of St Albans), Newark, Blyth, Doncaster, Pontefract, Boroughbridge, Northallerton and Durham. On map C the route continues north to Berwick, and on map D the route has Leicester on a branch route, the main route going via Stamford, and Newcastle is not shown (figure 15). Only on map D, which is just an unfinished sketch, are the towns actually connected by lines. Paris probably derived the route from a written itinerary and tried to fill in the rest of the country around it. The maps are crude and must be used with caution – a legend on map D disarmingly states that the island would have been elongated if the page size had been larger!

Much better evidence for the road system is to be found on the Gough map of about 1360, which depicts some 4730 km (2940 miles) of roads covering most of England. Part of the map appears on the cover of this book, and Cumbria is shown in figure 16. It is not known who drew the map; it is named after the antiquarian Richard Gough, who first described it in 1780. The interpretation of this map is made difficult because neither its purpose nor its sources are known, but it appears to have been an official compilation for government use, perhaps amended for use in certain areas – for example, the extant copy has networks of local roads in south-east Yorkshire and Lincolnshire. Distances are given between most towns, probably in old French miles (about $1^{1}/4$ statute miles or 2 km), and almost forty per cent of the routes shown are along the line of Roman roads.

Gough map: roads and distances
Main roads and branches

M1   London X Kingston V Cobham XV Guildford IX Farnham VII Alton VII Alresford VII Winchester XX Salisbury XVIII Shaftesbury XII Sherborne XX Crewkerne XII Chard XI Honiton XII Exeter XX Okehampton XVI (Launceston) XX Camelford XV Bodmin . . . St Columb XV St Ives

M2   London . . . Brentford XVII Colnbrook VII Maidenhead X Reading XV Newbury VII Hungerford VIII Marlborough XXX Chippenham XX Bristol

M2a   Reading XX Oxford

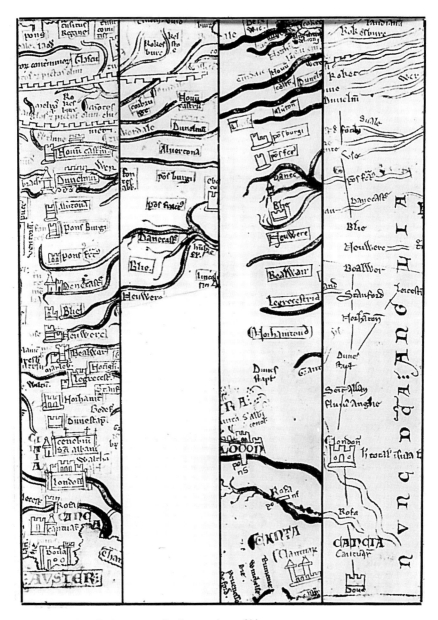

15. The Matthew Paris route on the four versions of his map.

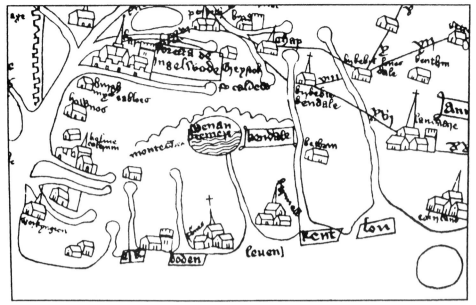

16. Gough map, Cumbria. This fourteenth-century map shows roads leading southwards from Carlisle; the area around London and south-east England appears on the front cover of this book.

M3　London XV Uxbridge XII High Wycombe X Tetsworth X Oxford X Witney VII Burford VIII Northleach XV Gloucester VII Newent XVII Hereford XII Clyro X Brecon X Llywel XVIII Langadock . . . Llandeilo X Carmarthen . . . St Clears XI Llawhaden VIII Haverfordwest VII St Davids

M3a　Oxford XII Faringdon XX Malmesbury XX Bristol

M3b　Oxford V Abingdon

M4　London X Barnet X St Albans X Dunstable VIII Stratford . . . Buckingham VI Towcester XII Daventry XVI Coventry VIII Coleshill XII Lichfield . . . Stone VI Newcastle-under-Lyme XXIIII Warrington VIII Wigan XII Preston XX Lancaster XVI Kendal XX Shap . . . Penrith XVI Carlisle

M4a　Stratford V Northampton XII Market Harborough XII Leicester

M4b　Stone . . . Stafford

M5　London XII Waltham Abbey VIII Ware XIII Royston IX Caxton VIII Huntingdon XIIII Ogerston V Wansford V Stamford XVI Grantham X Newark X Tuxford X Blyth VIII Doncaster X Pontefract XX Wetherby VIII Boroughbridge XIIII Leeming X Gilling X Bowes XIIII Brough XI Appleby X Penrith

M5a　Ware XII Barkway XII Cambridge X Newmarket X Bury St Edmunds X Thetford XXXII Norwich

M5b　Doncaster XIII Wakefield . . . Bradford . . . Skipton X Settle XII Kirkby Lonsdale VIII Kendal

M5c　Kirkby Lonsdale . . . Shap

Secondary roads and branches

S1　Southampton . . . Havant XXII Chichester X Arundel X Bramber X Lewes XVIII Boreham Street . . . Battle VII Winchelsea VIII Rye . . . Appledore XVII Canterbury

S2　Cardigan XXIII Aberystwyth XII Aberdovey XII Barmouth XI Llaneddwyn . . . Harlech XII Criccieth XXIIII Caernarvon VIII Bangor XV (Capel

	Curig) VIII Conwy . . . Abergele IIII Rhuddlan X Flint X Chester
S3	Bristol XV Newport XV Gloucester VIII Tewkesbury XIII Worcester X Droitwich XIIII Solihull VIII Coventry XVI Leicester X Melton Mowbray X Grantham
S3a	Droitwich X Birmingham X Lichfield XVI Derby XV Chesterfield XVI Doncaster
S3b	Worcester XII Kidderminster XII Bridgnorth XV Shrewsbury XII Ellesmere VII Overton XII Chester X Liverpool
S4	Bristol X(V?)
S5	Bristol XIII Axbridge
S6	Richmond X Bolton X Hawes X Sedbergh X Kirkby Lonsdale
S7	Bridport X Lyme

Local roads – Lincolnshire

L1	Lincoln XIIII Sleaford
L2	Lincoln XXVI Boston
L3	Lincoln X Spital-in-the-Street X Kirton . . . Brigg VIII Barton
L4	Barton XII Caistor XVI Horncastle V Bolingbroke IX Boston
L5	Boston XII Spalding
L6	Boston XII Wainfleet

Local roads – Yorkshire

Y1	Leeming XII Helperby X York
Y2	York XIIII Malton V Pickering
Y3	York X Pocklington VII Market Weighton
Y4	York XVI Market Weighton VIII Beverley
Y5	York XVI Howden
Y6	Beverley XVI Bridlington XII Scarborough XII Whitby XVII Guisborough

The map omits several well-known roads such as those from London to Dover and York to Newcastle, although it does show the towns en route correctly. The omission of the latter route is a particular puzzle, as it was much used as the main route to Scotland. Viewing the map as a whole, the sheer number of towns shown would enable the traveller to plan a journey, even if an actual route was not shown. Many places such as Bitchfield (between Stamford and Lincoln) and Bentham (between Settle and Lancaster) are included only because they were stages between larger towns. Overall the criteria for the choice of towns shown on the map remain a mystery. The roads do, however, reflect the centralisation of government, for there is clearly a national road system radiating from London, despite the fact that certain important towns, such as Plymouth, King's Lynn and Colchester, which were probably among the ten largest in size, are not connected to the network at all. York, the second largest town, is poorly served, and Lincoln has only local roads, although from here the normal route to York would have been by river.

It is tempting to presume that the lines marked on the map represented actual roads on the ground; this is probably true of routes that ran along Roman roads, although there are numerous examples of later roads

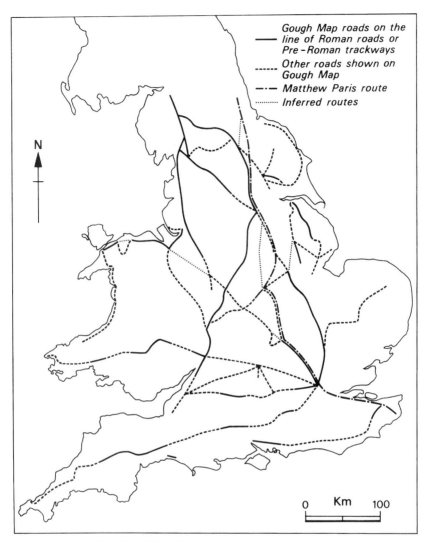

17. The routes of the Paris and Gough maps.

having developed alongside Roman roads because travellers shunned the hard surface (if it still survived) for the softer ground alongside. The routes that do not follow Roman roads must have been tracks which developed through the continual passage of traffic; at the very least they were directions on the map to guide the traveller across open country. The routes of Matthew Paris and the Gough map are shown on a modern map in figure 17.

5

Archaeological evidence

Whereas our knowledge of the Roman road system has always been strongly aided by archaeological evidence, the fact that medieval roads were not formally constructed or engineered makes any such line of investigation of them difficult. What remains of the field evidence is of two kinds: tracks and bridges. Tracks sometimes remain intact, especially where the land has not been ploughed. Even where tracks have gone across farmland they can often still be seen on aerial photographs, either as actual tracks or as crop marks. Figures 18 to 20 show three places where multiple tracks have been created as travellers chose the easiest way up a slope; these tracks have survived because they were never ploughed out. Figure 21 shows multiple tracks spreading out to over ten times the width of the present-day road, crossing relatively flat ground, whilst aerial photography is able to pick out features not visible from the ground in figure 22. The difficulty of dating a road is represented by figure 23, showing a road that has been in use for almost 2000 years. Figures 24 and 25 demonstrate the durability of the Roman road network, already a thousand years old by the medieval period.

On the ground the most impressive feature is the 'holloway' or sunken

18. Multiple tracks climb Postern Hill just south-east of Marlborough, Wiltshire.

19. Multiple tracks climb out of the Vale of Pewsey at Walkers Hill, near Alton Priors, Wiltshire.

20. Multiple tracks wend their way on to Rodborough Common, south of Stroud, Gloucester-shire.

21. Multiple tracks along Winsford Hill, Somerset.

22. Crop marks, invisible at ground level, cross a field near Ampleforth, North Yorkshire.

23. Gaddesden Row, Hertfordshire, is an example of a road in use for thousands of years, from prehistoric and Roman times through the medieval period to the present day.

24. The well preserved Roman road ascending Blackstone Edge, above Littleborough, near Manchester. Many Roman roads remained in use in medieval times.

25. Only a few metres from figure 24, the Blackstone Edge Roman road has disintegrated, yet its route still provides the easiest way across the moorland. Many Roman roads may have looked like this in medieval times.

26. The deeply entrenched holloway at Richard's Castle, on the Shropshire–Herefordshire border, near Ludlow.

road, found when a road descended a slope and became virtually a stream channel in times of heavy rain, deepened by as much as 3 to 6 metres (10 to 20 feet; figures 1, 26 and 27). For the rest, the field archaeologist has to be content with raised or sunken tracks across fields, or double lynchet ways

where a track was cut into a slope or hillside. It is rare to find a stretch of track more than a kilometre in length, and most are much shorter, leaving a host of disjointed local tracks, many of which may or may not have been in use in the middle ages. One always has to return to the documentary sources to see whether any particular road was in use in medieval times.

27. The steep holloway at Richard's Castle is some 5 metres (16 feet) deep.

28. The deserted medieval village of More, near Bishop's Castle, Shropshire, has a road leading from the motte (top) to the present-day road (bottom).

Deserted medieval villages are perhaps the one exception to this rule, for in such cases part of the medieval landscape has been fossilised, and old routes which are no longer used can be identified. Figure 28 shows the village of More in Shropshire, which was created out of the neighbouring parish of Lydham in the early twelfth century. It was a defended village, being close to the Welsh border and in a valley which must have seen Welsh incursions. The village thus had a motte and a ringwork, and clear traces of house platforms and roads can still be seen today both from the air and on the ground. The village decayed to its present size of a church and a handful of houses in the sixteenth century, so in this case the road is medieval in date and of no other period.

Bridges and causeways, however, attracted more attention than roads in medieval times. Their provision and maintenance was regarded as a pious act, and consequently church records often refer to them. Special taxes (pontages) were sometimes raised for their upkeep, and they figure more often than roads in medieval court cases. Medieval bridges were simple at first, being wide enough only for packhorses; there was usually a ford alongside for wagons. Stone bridges are numerous, the earliest being about 1180; they include a thirteenth-century one at Castle Combe (Wiltshire) and the one *c.*1500 at Sutton (Bedfordshire; figure 29). Even in remote Westmorland (now part of Cumbria), twelve stone

29. Sutton packhorse bridge, Bedfordshire, is a massively built structure, dating from *c.*1400. Its total span is 8.2 metres (27 feet), and there is a ford alongside.

30. This nineteenth-century photograph shows the medieval bridge with its gate tower guarding entry into the town of Warkworth, Northumberland.

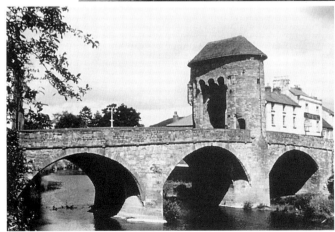

31. The medieval bridge at the south-west entrance to the town of Monmouth.

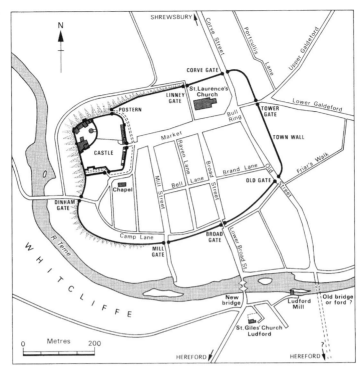

32. In early medieval Ludlow, the main road through the Welsh Marches ran along Corve Street and Old Street and crossed the river Teme at a ford. In the early thirteenth century a new bridge was built, and traffic diverted through the centre of the town, down Broad Street.

bridges are known to have existed in the fourteenth century.

A few towns had fortified bridges; examples still survive at Warkworth (Northumberland; figure 30) and Monmouth (figure 31). Large bridges were needed in many places, especially near towns and on the major routes, for example at Staines and Windsor on the main road west from London and on the Welsh border road at Ludlow. The whole development of the latter town was altered when new streets were laid out and a new bridge built. The town grew originally between the castle, which is on a rocky promontory above the river, and the main north-south route through the Marches; this junction (the Bull Ring) formed one end of a large market area, now much infilled (figure 32). The town grew around the market area and on either side of the north–south route (Corve Street and Old Street), until a large extension to the town was laid out in the thirteenth century and the traffic was diverted through the market and down Broad Street to the new bridge over the river Teme. The road to Hereford, south of the river, was also diverted some distance to the west.

Perhaps the best-known example of where a new bridge altered the course of a road as well as the fortunes of a whole town is where the

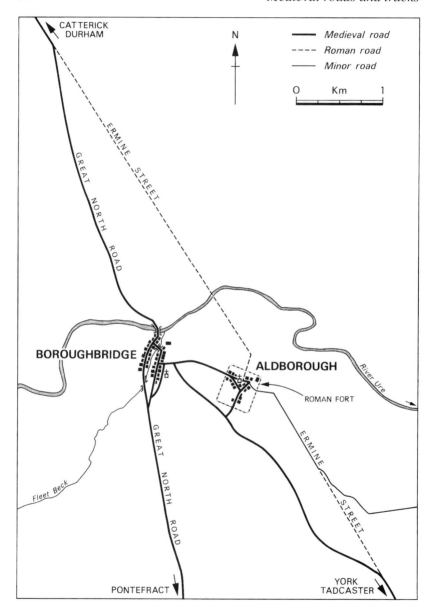

33. The Great North Road at Boroughbridge was diverted from the line of the Roman Ermine Street to a new bridge, which led to the decline of Aldborough.

Great North Road crosses the Ure (figure 33). Formerly the Roman road crossed near what is now Aldborough (North Yorkshire), but the building of a new bridge in the early twelfth century shifted the route 800 metres (^{1}/2 mile) to the west, and the new town of Boroughbridge grew up there. The road which used to lead from Aldborough to the river Ure degenerated into a grassy lane and finally ceased to be a road altogether when the village was enclosed in 1809.

The building of Harnham Bridge south of the new town of Salisbury in 1244 diverted traffic from Wilton, which had formerly been the major town in the area. Equally, the building of the bridge at Abingdon probably contributed to the decline of Dorchester on Thames and even Wallingford. One of the finest medieval bridges is at Newbridge in Oxfordshire (figure 34).

Some causeways were quite substantial: Holland Bridge near Boston (Lincolnshire) was 3 metres (10 feet) broad and 2.4 metres (8 feet) high, having thirty bridges in one section. Maud Heath's causeway, which runs for 7 km (4^1/2 miles) near Chippenham (Wiltshire), was built as a legacy in 1474 to enable people to cross the river Avon dryshod. The fen causeways to Ely are clearly the largest examples in England.

34. Newbridge has the finest medieval bridge in Oxfordshire, at the confluence of the Thames and the Windrush. It has pointed arches and strongly projecting cutwaters.

6

Studies of individual roads

Studies of medieval roads on the small scale have tended to look either at roads within a single parish, usually where an early map survives, or at one particular route, which may have surviving earthworks. In their aerial survey of medieval England, Beresford and St Joseph choose the village of Padbury (Buckinghamshire) to study in some detail, having already looked at its fields and the effects of enclosure. Their starting point is an Elizabethan plan of the parish dated 1591 (figure 35). This shows a radial network of seven lanes with branches and cross routes, leading from the village street out into the fields. Most of them degenerate into smaller tracks, including the one named 'Buckingham Waye' which led to the county town, less than 5 km (3 miles) distant. The other route named as heading for a specific place, 'Whadden Waye', made its way across the fields for almost 10 km (6 miles) to Whaddon, but this route is now only a footpath. Such local roads were of vital importance to the needs of the village; they led out to the fields and to outlying woods, pasture or mills. They were irregular in both direction and width, and few continued even to the parish boundary, let alone to adjoining villages.

In areas of more dispersed settlement, away from the typical compact villages and open fields of midland England, the road network is totally different, with lanes linking one isolated farm to the next – though again there were comparatively few direct routes between villages, which were, in any case, far apart. Such patterns are well represented in the south-western counties of England.

Virtually the whole rural landscape of England has been altered since medieval times by the enclosure of the open fields. Whereas medieval roads had some degree of freedom to move or spread out, the new enclosure roads were made straighter and were confined by walls or hedges. Unfortunately, few detailed pre-enclosure maps survive, so it is difficult to see how the pattern of roads has changed unless the land has remained largely undisturbed by deep ploughing, thus allowing the medieval field tracks to survive. These can often be seen on aerial photographs, sometimes with the former road network totally separate from the present-day one (figure 28).

Examples of the way in which a medieval road would spread out over a large area are best seen where the road left cultivated land, and in particular where it had to climb a hill and was able to diverge over common or waste land. Examples include Rodborough Common near Stroud (Gloucestershire), Walkers Hill near Alton (Wiltshire) and Postern

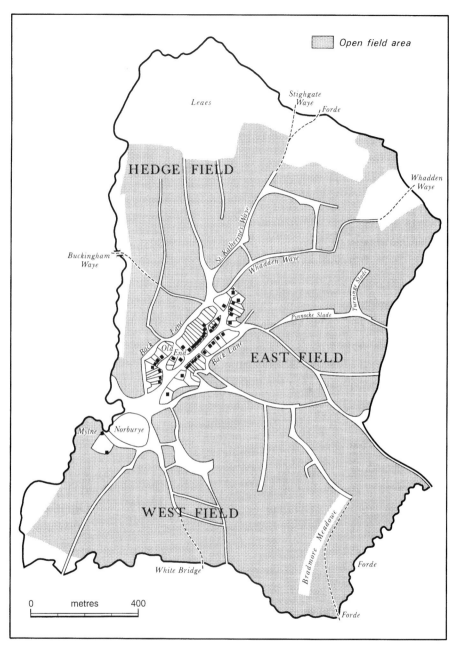

Open field area

Leaes

Stighgate
Waye
Forde

Whadden
Waye

HEDGE FIELD

St. Katherine's Waye

Whadden Waye

Buckingham
Waye

Turning Stall

Pinnocke Slade

Back Lane

Back Lane

Old End

EAST FIELD

Mylne

Norburye

WEST FIELD

Bradmore Meadowe

Forde

0   metres   400

White Bridge

Forde

35. Local roads in medieval Padbury, Buckinghamshire, based on a sixteenth-century map of the village. Note the irregular nature of the local roads and how few reach the parish boundary.

36. An oblique aerial photograph of multiple tracks on Twyford Down east of Winchester, Hampshire. The road still in use was a Roman road.

Hill near Marlborough (Wiltshire; figures 18-20). In figures 36 and 37 showing Twyford Down near Winchester (Hampshire), it is possible to see the road leaving the cultivated land of the Itchen valley as it makes its way south, just outside Winchester, to join a ridgeway to the South

37. Holloway tracks on Twyford Down. This part of the down is very close to the controversial M3.

38. Multiple tracks descending from Beacon Hill, Bulford, Wiltshire, towards the crossing of the river Avon.

Downs and to link the county town directly with the bishop's palace at Waltham and the boroughs of Portchester and Portsmouth. The tracks branch out to climb the 60 metres (200 feet) of Deacon Hill just below the iron age ramparts of St Catherine's Hill. There is still a modern track climbing the hill directly, but the present road swings round to the east to take the hill more gently.

Figure 38 shows Beacon Hill, about 12 km (1½ miles) east of Amesbury in Wiltshire. Here the London to Bath road descends some 80 metres (270 feet) from Beacon Hill, towards the crossing of the river Avon at Bulford. This route has now been rendered obsolete by a newer crossing of the Avon, further south at Amesbury. There are numerous other examples throughout England, but they are limited in length and the date of such tracks cannot be known for certain.

Roads were important in determining the success or otherwise of towns and their markets; many of the towns which failed were simply not well located with respect to the road system. At Brough in Cumbria, for example, a castle was built in about 1100 on the site of an old Roman fort (figure 39). The foundation failed to prosper, however, because markets were held 600 metres (⅓ mile) further north at Market Brough, which was sited on a medieval diversion of the Roman road

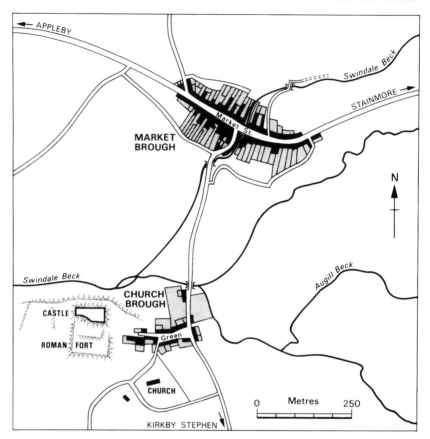

39. Medieval Brough shows the effect of the diversion of the road on the settlement. The Roman road had been some 600 metres south of the medieval road, but the diversion created the new settlement of Market Brough.

descending from Stainmore, on its way to Appleby, Penrith and Carlisle. In Ludlow, as outlined in chapter 5, the main road, a river crossing and a planned extension to the town all affected each other.

Studies of individual routes are rare; but C. Taylor has studied several routes in the east Midlands (figure 40). The first is the road from Stamford (Lincolnshire) to Kettering (Northamptonshire). In this case various subsequent diversions can be seen both in the villages and in the fields en route. In particular there is a fine holloway some 1.8 metres (6 feet) deep and 10.7 metres (35 feet) wide south of Bulwick; this runs parallel to the modern road for most of the way to Deenethorpe, where the

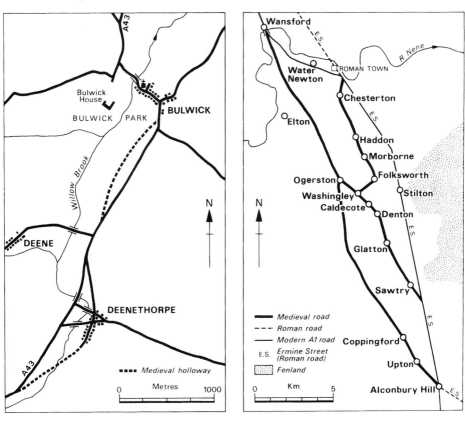

40. Two medieval routes in the east Midlands. (After C. Taylor.)

medieval road leads into the village, and is represented by a holloway once again south of the cul-de-sac in the village.

A short distance to the south-east, in Cambridgeshire, Taylor gives a somewhat more complex example showing the changes in a route from Roman times to the present day, where the Roman road was probably abandoned in favour of drier routes further west, most of which have, in their turn, been abandoned, at least as through routes. The main medieval road from Wansford went by way of Coppingford and Ogerston to Alconbury. Ogerston was a medieval manor, and although a farm is all that remains today it is marked on the Gough map as the stage between Huntingdon and Wansford. Another medieval route leaves Ermine Street near Sawtry, also trying to avoid the fenlands; each of the villages

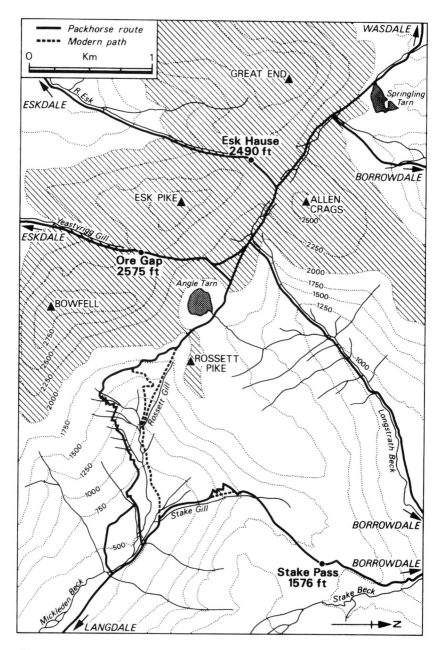

41. Tracks and passes at the head of Langdale, Cumbria, leading towards Wasdale and Borrowdale.

42. Rossett Gill and Esk Hause, Cumbria. The old packhorse track (A–A–A) keeps well clear of the steep and stony bed of the gill. The modern zigzag (B) can also be seen.

through which this route passes is laid out along it, even though it is now represented only by a disjointed set of lanes and paths. Finally there is evidence to suggest that the Roman road had come back into use later in the medieval period.

Any fell walker in the Lake District will be familiar with the zigzag paths that wend their way up most of the passes from Nan Bield in the

43. Part of the zigzag track on Stake Pass, Cumbria, taken before it was reinstated in the 1980s.

east to Sty Head in the west. Again it is difficult to date these tracks, but their earliest use was probably medieval, even though they were not causeyed or surfaced in any way until the sixteenth century at the earliest. As trade increased the elaborate zigzag routes were constructed to ease the gradients of the mountain passes for the packhorses. The modern hiker in haste normally ignores these, and thus they usually survive. Two good examples can be found close together at the head of Langdale: Stake Pass climbs north towards Borrowdale, and Rossett Gill has its packhorse route well away from the steep and stony climb of the gill itself (figures 41 to 43). Furness Abbey, situated in the extreme southwest of Cumbria, had lands in upper Eskdale (near Hardknott) and also in Borrowdale some 13 km (8 miles) further north, across some of the highest land in England. One of the passes between them is called Ore Gap, and it was certainly used for the movement of iron ore in medieval times, albeit in small quantities.

There are many books that deal with individual routes at a local or county level, but they all struggle with the problem of dating the roads and hence, to a greater or lesser degree, have difficulty dealing with the period between the departure of the Romans and the coming of the turnpikes. The series of books published by Moorland and Cicerone Press covers five areas in England and Wales (see Select Bibliography).

7

The road network

Very few attempts have been made to look beyond individual roads or parishes to try to establish what the medieval road network was like. The present author has made a study of the roads of the medieval diocese of Carlisle, which is fortunate in having the itinerary of Bishop John de Halton (1292-1324) to help in a reconstruction of the road system. This chapter will look at Cheshire, as this county is a particularly interesting case, and then at the whole of England and Wales.

Cheshire

While this short study cannot hope to be definitive because of the lack of detailed field evidence, it will show how the various historical sources can be used. The first step is to establish the Roman road network – though the precise route of large sections of it is uncertain, notably the route from Chester to Wilderspool (figure 44).

Also shown on figure 44 are the locations of place-names with elements that suggest the existence of a road; they include *ford, bridge, street* and *stretton* and the Welsh elements *cryw* (ford), *ffordd* or *heol* (road) and *sarn* (causeway). These place-names appear again in figure 45, where, by a process of connecting each one to its nearest neighbour and looking in detail at the alignments of the villages and their roads, it is possible to piece together several 'linear routes', one of which is along the Chester to Wilderspool route. D. Sylvester has also suggested three other routes in the east of the county that have been partly identified in the field.

Cheshire was important commercially for its salt production, and there are several 'saltways' linking the 'wiches' to various 'salt' place-names. Saltways were not special roads, and the far-flung 'salt' place-names are connected by roads known to have been in use either in the medieval period or later. Place-names are only of limited value, principally because they do not give a date to a road and often refer to pre-medieval roads. More useful are the royal itineraries, and the travels of Edward I and Henry III are plotted in figure 46. Many of the routes taken by the monarchs follow known roads, but some do not, for example those between Ince and Vale Royal and between Macclesfield and Nantwich. Edward's route to Overton probably matched that shown in the Gough map. Few of the routes used by the kings follow place-name roads: only those from Nantwich to Combermere and from Barnshaw to Macclesfield do so. The Gough map roads are also shown in figure 46, including the main road to the north, which passes through the county

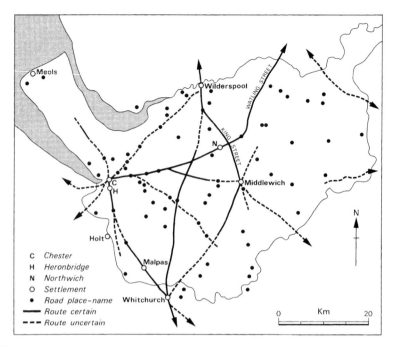

44. Roman roads and road place-names in Cheshire.

45. Medieval routes in Cheshire.

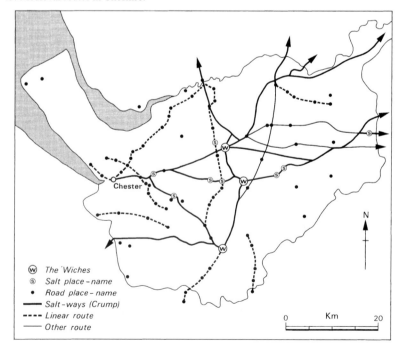

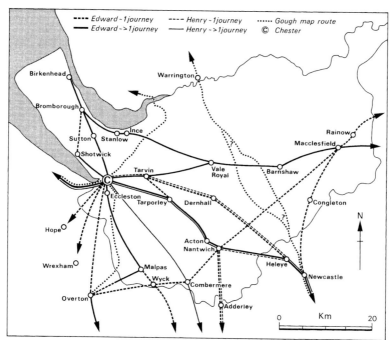

46. Royal itineraries in Cheshire.

from Newcastle-under-Lyme to Warrington, but although two intermediate places are shown its precise route is uncertain. The other Gough map route was from Shrewsbury and divided at Chester to go into north Wales and Liverpool. Again, its precise course can only be guessed at.

Chester was an important town in medieval England. Although it probably had a population of just over two thousand for most of the period, its lack of growth caused it to fall from being the fourth largest borough in England in 1086 to forty-second largest in 1348. Nevertheless, it would have had strong links and good roads to other towns, including Shrewsbury, York and London.

In such local studies it is also sometimes useful to use post-medieval evidence, but only to confirm the existence of earlier roads. The earliest of such sources usually dates from the sixteenth or seventeenth century, and the roads given by Harrison, Smith, Ogilby and Morden at various dates between 1586 and 1695 are plotted on figure 47.

A synthesis of all this information, together with much detailed fieldwork, would lead us nearer a depiction of the medieval roads of Cheshire. As it stands, this cartographic approach has left many unresolved problems, in particular the routes taken by the Gough map roads and the general confusion around Middlewich and Nantwich. In

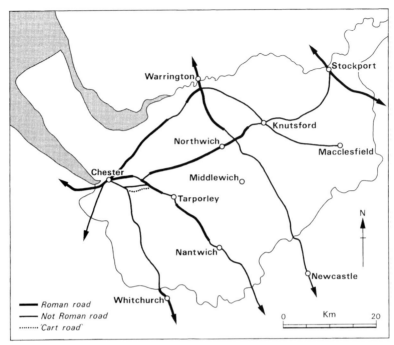

47. Post-medieval map routes in Cheshire.

some areas parallel lines of travel follow each other over considerable distances, and there appears to be no major route into Wales from the southern half of the county. Nonetheless, the maps show the importance of Chester and the main route from Newcastle-under-Lyme to Warrington. On the other hand the 'wiches' are surprisingly poorly connected, although they are all linked to Chester, which may have been an important distribution centre. A generally flat county such as Cheshire would present few obstacles to travel, which no doubt accounts for much of the proliferation of routes.

This short study of Cheshire is intended to show how all the sources and methods mentioned earlier can be applied to an area the size of a county, and there is a need for more research at this level. It is possible at this scale to build up a broader picture than can be obtained by looking solely at one road.

England and Wales

Any attempt to build a national picture of the road network must be speculative, but there is considerable evidence to show which were the

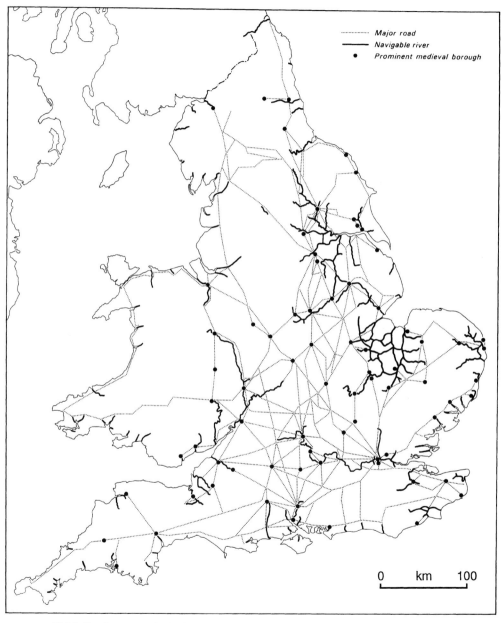

48. Medieval routes and principal towns in England and Wales.

most important routes. The starting point must be the Roman road system, large parts of which were clearly still in use, as shown by the Gough map and the royal itineraries, despite the ravages of time and weather since the departure of the Romans. Indeed their routes have survived, and many are still in use today, though not always as through routes. To this can be added the evidence of roads on contemporary maps and the major routes used by the kings that were not along Roman routes, all of which could, in a sense, be described as the medieval roads that made and maintained themselves.

This distinction between the two types of road is especially apparent in certain areas; Cirencester is an important junction in the Roman system, yet Oxford and Windsor are totally divorced from it. Other distinctions emerge too: Oxford is an important junction on the map evidence, but the itineraries give more prominence to the palace of Woodstock, 13 km (8 miles) to the north. The principal centre is clearly London, followed, in order, by York, Marlborough, Leicester, Salisbury, Winchester, Woodstock, Lincoln, Chester, Shrewsbury, Lichfield, Gloucester, Oxford and Windsor. This network is clearly at its best in central and southern England and poor in all the surrounding areas.

Research by Jim Edwards has shown that river transport in medieval times was more important than many had previously thought. Of the major rivers, the Severn was navigated to Welshpool, the Thames to Lechlade, the Trent to Burton, and the Yorkshire Ouse and Swale to Richmond. It was also possible to navigate from the Trent at Torksey along the Foss Dyke to Lincoln, and thence down the Whitham to Boston. The numerous rivers of eastern England, notably around the fens, plus those flowing into the Humber, allowed heavy or bulky cargoes to be moved conveniently by water. Relatively few parts of the country were more than 25 km (15 miles) or so from navigable water, and thus the rivers formed part of the overall transport system (figure 48). Urban growth clearly relied on trade, and of the most populous towns, only Coventry was not on navigable water; others such as Winchester and Thetford declined in importance, due at least in part to the difficulties of reaching them by boat. The contrast can be seen clearly in the Welsh borders where Shrewsbury on the Severn grew dramatically whilst Ludlow, on the unnavigable Teme, did not. Nevertheless, the road system still remained the basic means of transport for most goods.

8
Tracing medieval roads

Whilst the chief excitement of tracing medieval roads always lies in trying to follow their course across the countryside, one first has to do a good deal of vital and significant groundwork in the library. The first step is to obtain an up-to-date, reliable and accurate map of Roman roads in the area you intend to study. The Ordnance Survey's *Map of Roman Britain* certainly does not show all the known or presumed roads, and recent research has not always been brought together even at a county scale. Usually you will have to search through local archaeological journals, and the county record office, museum or local history library should be of great help, both with references and with putting you in touch with the local expert on Roman roads.

When you have established the probable Roman road network, the next step is to see how much of it was used in medieval times, and then to see where new roads had come into use. This requires searching through the map evidence, whether it be the Gough map or later local or county maps, and using large-scale Ordnance Survey maps – the 1:25,000 Pathfinder series and the older 6 inch (1:10,560) are ideal – as a base on which to plot all the available information. These maps also show a vast number of place-names, which can reveal old routes. Local charters may mention roads; the local bishop may have granted indulgences to anyone repairing roads or bridges (usually the dates of construction of bridges are known); and travellers from the king downwards may have left records. In particular the itinerary of Edward I is well worth consulting (see chapter 3).

Your county record office and local history library are the best places to start research. Because of the difficulties of dating a road in the field, it is much better to do all the documentary research first and then move on to look for any physical remains. Air photographs are especially useful. Probably the best collection of these is that in the University of Cambridge, which is classified by both subject (for our purpose 'Ancient roads') and parish; most parishes in England and Wales are covered, and because old tracks show up best from the air, especially with low sunlight, the study of aerial photographs is often more rewarding than trying to trace the same feature in the field.

Finally, armed with all the available documentary and cartographic evidence, you can go into the field to see what, if anything, remains of medieval roads and, above all, to see more clearly what options were open to the traveller in medieval England. There is a desperate need for further research at the local and county level to discover exactly what did happen to the roads of England in the twelve hundred years between the departure of the Romans and the creation of the first turnpike roads in the seventeenth and eighteenth centuries.

9
Select bibliography

Roads and landscapes
Aston, M. *Interpreting the Landscape.* Batsford, 1985.
Cantor, L. (editor). *The English Medieval Landscape.* Croom Helm, 1982.
Hindle, B.P. *Maps for Historians.* Phillimore, 1998.
Hindle, B.P. *Roads and Tracks for Historians.* Phillimore, 2001.

Medieval roads
Beresford, M.W., and St Joseph, J.K.S. *Medieval England – An Aerial Survey.* Cambridge University Press, 1979.
Flower, C.T. 'Public Works in Medieval Law', *Seldon Society,* 32 (1915) and 40 (1923).
Gough, H. *Itinerary of King Edward the First.* 1900.
Hallam, E.M. 'The Itinerary of Edward II and His Household', *List and Index Society,* 211 (1984).
Hindle, B.P. 'The Road Network of Medieval England and Wales', *Journal of Historical Geography,* 2 (1976), pages 207-21.
Hindle, B.P. 'Seasonal Variations in Travel in Medieval England', *Journal of Transport History,* 4 (1978), pages 170-8.
Hindle, B.P. 'The Towns and Roads of the Gough Map', *The Manchester Geographer,* 1 (1980), pages 35-49.
Hindle, B.P., and Edwards, J.F. 'The Transportation System of Medieval England and Wales', *Journal of Historical Geography,* 17/2 (1991), pages 123-34 (see also 19/1 (1993), pages 12-14).
Jusserand, J.J. *English Wayfaring Life in the Middle Ages.* 1884.
Martin, G.H. 'Road Travel in the Middle Ages', *Journal of Transport History,* 3 (1976), pages 159-78.
Parsons, E.J.S. *The Map of Great Britain c. AD 1360, Known as the Gough Map.* Bodleian Library, 1958.

Local studies
Colyer, R. *Roads and Trackways of Wales.* Moorland, 1984.
Dodd, A.E. and E.M. *Peakland Roads and Trackways.* Moorland, 1980.
Hemery, E. *Walking Dartmoor's Ancient Tracks.* Hale,1986.
Hindle, B.P. *Roads and Tracks of the Lake District.* Cicerone Press, 1998.
Jennett, S. *The Pilgrims' Way.* Cassell,1971.
Robertson, A.E. *Old Tracks, Cross-country Routes and 'Coffin Roads' in the North-west Highlands.* Scottish Mountaineering Club Journal, 1947.
Toulson, S. *The Moors of the Southwest:* (1) *Exploring the Ancient Tracks of Sedgemoor and Exmoor,* Hutchinson,1983; (2) *Exploring the Ancient Tracks of Dartmoor, Bodmin and Penwith,* Hutchinson,1984.
Wright, G.N. *Roads and Trackways of the Yorkshire Dales.* Moorland, 1985.
Wright, G.N. *Roads and Trackways of Wessex.* Moorland, 1988.

Index